Needlerush, Juncus roemerianus, *dominates large areas of the Dorchester marshes.*

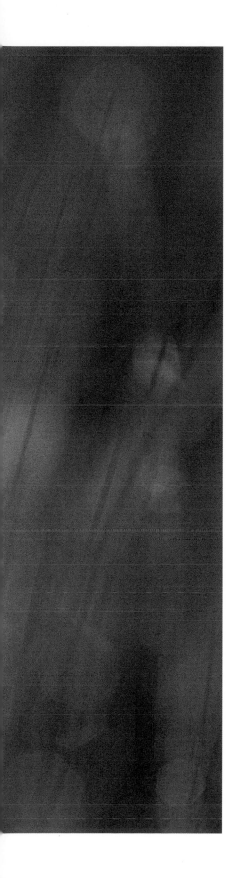

OPPOSITE: *Droplets of water from morning dew are highlighted by the rising sun in a salt marsh. Walking through a needlerush marsh is a wet and prickly experience.*

The rising sea level and the eroding effects of windblown water are rapidly destroying James Island off the mouth of the Little Choptank River.

ABOVE: *Donald Mills sews together lengths of nylon net to make a pound net for a local fisherman.*

Morning mists rise from a timbered area along the Nanticoke River.

David W. Harp and Tom Horton

The GREAT MARSH

An Intimate Journey into a Chesapeake Wetland

The Johns Hopkins University Press   *Baltimore & London*

© 2002 The Johns Hopkins University Press

All rights reserved. Published 2002

Printed in Hong Kong on acid-free paper

9 8 7 6 5 4 3 2 1

The Johns Hopkins University Press

2715 North Charles Street

Baltimore, Maryland 21218-4363

www.press.jhu.edu

TITLE PAGE: Tidal flow from Hopkins Cove pushes up into a marsh of needle rush, spartina grasses and loblolly pines near Crocheron.

Library of Congress Cataloging-in-Publication Data

Harp, David W.

The great marsh: an intimate journey into a Chesapeake wetland / David W. Harp and Tom Horton.

p.   cm.

ISBN 0-8018-6777-0 (hardcover: alk. paper)

1. Natural history—Maryland—Blackwater National Wildlife Refuge. 2. Wetland ecology—Maryland—Blackwater National Wildlife Refuge. 3. Blackwater National Wildlife Refuge (Md.)—Pictorial works. I. Horton, Tom, 1945– II. Title.

QH105.M3 H37 2002

508.752'27—dc21

2001001762

A catalog record for this book is available from the British Library.

This book is dedicated to
Don Baugh, who has
inspired and led so many
Chesapeake journeys.

Preface

THE WRITER AND PHOTOGRAPHER hard at work: first day of autumn, cool and sunny, time to launch the kayak and paddle for hours, looking for whatever's about in the Eastern Shore marshes. Today, Monarchs rule. The brilliant butterflies are migrating through on their way from Maine to Mexico—so thick they literally coat bushes and branches where they pause to rest. A cell-phone call from water's edge soon has Dave Harp en route from Baltimore, a hundred miles away. We've spent half our lives, it seems, kicking around the marshy Chesapeake fringes and have never seen such a sight. Before dawn the next morning we're camped by a choice "butterfly bush," photographing as the rising sun kindles it to glowing, quivering, fluttering life. Officially, we were there working on this book. But of course we've been enjoying ourselves this way long before, and will continue long afterward. The marsh has been our work and our playground. Often it's hard to separate the two; and as we sought out and photographed trappers, archaeologists, fishermen, and naturalists, that seemed the case also with them.

Historically, wetlands—a modern term not coined until the 1950s—covered 11 percent of the continental United States. Draining and filling have reduced that to 5 percent, and many of those wetlands are degraded in quality. Maryland was once one-quarter wetlands and now is about one-fifteenth. But the old notions of "swamps," places both "dismal" and "malarial," are being replaced by descriptors like *kidneys*, *gills*, and *lungs*. These acknowledge scientific evidence that wetlands contribute immensely to filtering pollution, retaining floodwaters, and recharging drinking-water aquifers—all in addition to their rich habitat values for marine

OPPOSITE: *The straight lines of manmade mosquito ditches contrast with the natural meanders of the marsh.*

and bird life. To comprehend in all its splendors the Great Marsh, as we came to call the subject of this book, one must see it through a variety of lenses, well beyond those in the photographer's bag. Trapper Robby Willey was ever patient in sharing his unique viewpoint as we slogged through miles of marsh while he checked his muskrat and nutria traps and joined him, his daughter Samantha, and his wife, Anne, in their skinning hut. Archaeologists Darren Lowery and Bruce Thompson gave us insight into the near and distant past by walking the edges of Dorchester County creeks and by raising a cen-turies-old log canoe from the muck of the Blackwater River. Pound netter Charles Wood-land welcomed us aboard his boat long before sunup to follow him from net to net in Fishing Bay, and Donald Mills showed us the nearly lost art of pound-net making in his front yard near Crocheron.

Don Jackson was always ready with skiff or canoe or kayak to show us the swans on Mar-shyhope Creek, to search for wood ducks on Chicone Creek, or to hunt with his Labrador retriever, Lucy, along Island Creek. We spent an extraordinary morning trotlining on Fox Creek and the Honga River with Elihu Abbott, and enjoyed a cup of coffee with him and his wife, Doris, at their home near Shorter's Wharf on more than one occasion. Diane Stoecker, a researcher at the University of Maryland Center for Environmental and Estuarine Studies at Horn Point, was always helpful during repeated attempts to capture the teeming life in a drop of marsh water through one of her high-tech microscopes. Nick Goetz and Matt Mullen, educators at the Chesapeake Bay Foundation's Karen Noonan Center at Bishops Head were helpful with weather and tide information as we planned forays into their far corner of the Great Marsh. Glen Carowan and Bill Geise were generous with their time and with access to the Blackwater National Wildlife Refuge.

We are especially grateful to two people who are no strangers to the Dorchester marshes, Turney McKnight of the Sumner T. McKnight Foundation and Blaine Phillips of the Fair Play Foundation, for their support of this project. Continued good fishing and hunting to them, for helping us share our marsh with a wider audience.

SPRING: *The First Voyage*

FIVE CENTURIES AFTER VERRAZANO discovered Chesapeake Bay, four centuries after John Smith charted it, was it still possible to make a voyage of discovery here in Maryland, the nation's fifth most densely settled state? The idea had grown from staring at a wall one cold winter week in an old hunting lodge in the marshy heart of Dorchester County.

On the wall, covering more than a hundred square feet, someone had fit together nearly a dozen beautifully detailed "quad," or quadrangle, maps to show in its entirety what David Harp and I had come to call the Great Marsh. It dominates the half of Maryland's largest county that lies south of U.S. Route 50, stretching, west to east, from Cambridge to Vienna, from Choptank to Nanticoke. It is a water-land of tidal rivers with haunting names—Honga, Transquaking, Blackwater, Chicamacomico, Marshy-

hope. Their sparsely developed banks would still be familiar to the Indians who once plied them in log canoes.

It is also a place of islands—Bloodsworth, Holland, Spring, Hooper, and Taylors—and long, lonesome "necks," peninsulas where minimal roadways and narrow bridges thread together isolated communities like Crapo, Crocheron, Elliott, Robbins, Bestpitch, and Bishops Head; where World's End Creek flows off to the horizon through Hell Hook Marsh. Kussawarook, or Tidewater People, was what the Indians of the Great Marsh encountered by John Smith in 1607 called themselves. Otayachgo, for People Who Built Bridges, the Mohicans called them. Where tidewater and the prairie-like salt marsh leave off, trackless forested swamps—Kentuck, Moneystump, Greenbrier, and Beechground—hold sway over the southern Dorchester interior.

OPPOSITE: *Kayaking is one of the best ways to explore the endless contours of the marsh edge.*

Morning sunlight explodes in a cloud of fog along Chicone Creek.

OPPOSITE: *Pesky gnats commonly known as "no-see-ums" shimmer in the horizontal rays of the sun on an early summer morning in Greenbrier Swamp.*

The wall of quad maps, derived from aerial photography but artistically illustrated, portrayed all this as a landscape of every shade and mix and texture of greens and blues, land and water mingled as intricately as anywhere on earth. And the closer we looked, connecting the meandering threads of water from river to pond to slough, the more it seemed that a "northwest passage," paddling some sixty miles through the whole of Maryland's largest county, might be possible. Local fishermen and hunters told us over the next several months that this piece and that of the voyage was doable. And we had heard intriguing rumors that were confirmed by officials of the Blackwater National Wildlife Refuge.

A rising sea level, just in the last decade or so, had literally been dissolving a marsh that for thousands of years had separated the Little

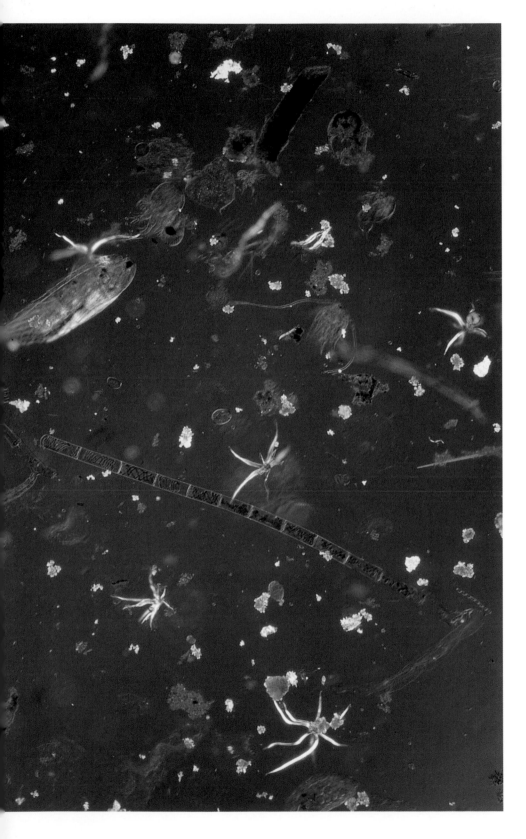

Beginnings of the food web: phytoplankton, zooplankton, and detritus share the confined space of a few drops of water from the Choptank River.

Choptank and the Blackwater River drainages. Potentially this opened the last obstacle to a through trip. The jumbled, fractured marsh that constituted much of the route meant we would seldom follow a straight line. But that is why inveterate marsh muckers, who understand that the straightest line between two points is never the most interesting, find the Great Marsh almost paradise (a zillion biting insects keep it "almost").

"The Chesapeake's Everglades," local ornithologist Paul Spitzer once dubbed southern Dorchester, which contains nearly 40 percent of all the tidal wetlands found in Maryland. Only 270,000 of the county's 630,000 acres is dry land; the rest is wetland and open water, sparsely studded with islands of loblolly pine that from a distance seem to float on the horizon. It is country that delights the eye and stretches the mind's horizons, a place of boundless space

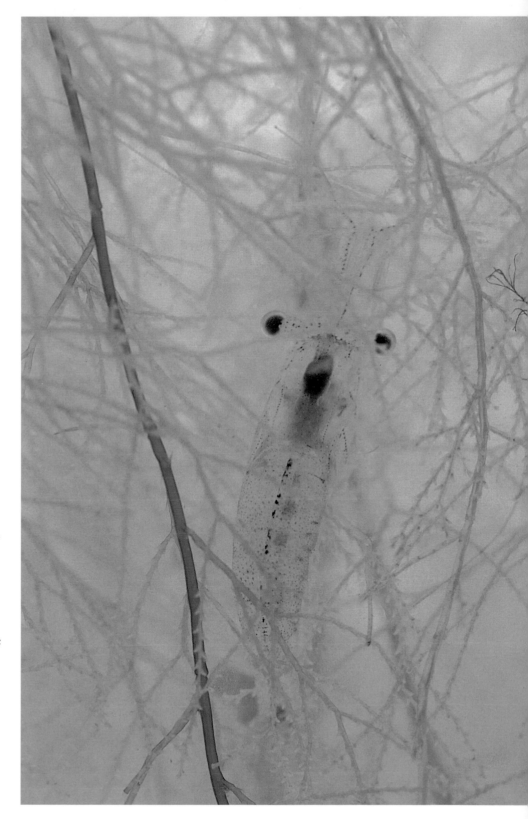

Looking more like a space alien than an inch-long grass shrimp (Palaemonetes pugio), this shallow-water inhabitant has little to hide with its transparent body. Grass shrimp are abundant in the aquatic vegetation of the shallows.

and light, vistas of rippling gold and green beneath a dome of sky, spread wantonly to the caresses of sun and moon and wind. All is riven with thousands of miles of watery meanders that continuously, sensuously entice one around the next bend.

It is simultaneously a traveler's challenge, with large stretches neither quite liquid enough for even small boat passage nor substantial enough for portaging; and this tenuous situation can swiftly worsen or improve from high tide to low and from southwest winds that pile tide upon tide to northerly blasts that blow immense volumes of water out of the Chesapeake. But the prospect that it might now be possible to paddle an uninterrupted east-west transect through the Great Marsh was enough to banish concerns about getting lost or stranded.

The standard value of wetlands, their immense productivity, is well known these days. The Dorchester marshes produce as much as eight thousand pounds of plant matter per acre per year, with no need for human inputs of labor, fuel, or fertilizer. Indeed, because they need nothing, clumsy human economic indicators assign no value to the work that wetlands perform. What an accounting error that is, as bacteria and tides swiftly translate their prodigious quantities of plant detritus into the aquatic food web, where its energy may pass through tiny floating plankton, into smaller and larger fish, and into the belly of a swooping

OPPOSITE: *A damsel fly clings to a stalk of black needlerush* (Juncus rocmerianus) *in a salt marsh near Crocheron. Needlerush, which is found in areas occasionally flooded by high tides, lives in close association with other salt-marsh grasses like* Spartina patens *and* Distichlis spicata.

A delight to the canoeist or kayaker, this tidal creek winds its way through a salt marsh and connects with Fishing Bay near Elliott's Island.

First light of the day trans-
forms a dew-laden spider
web into a crown jewel in
a marsh near Bestpitch
Ferry.

A school bus affords its passengers a lovely view of loblolly pine, marsh, and sky as it approaches the Blackwater River at Shorter's Wharf.

Ground fog caused by cool air flowing over warmer land and water creeps across farmland and marsh along the upper Nanticoke River.

The large flower of a hibiscus plant blooms along Elliott's Island Road.

eagle or osprey in a matter of hours. Less quantifiable, but no less important, is the license such large, untrammeled spaces as the Great Marsh offer travelers-through to imagine, to let the mind run free in a way it cannot do amid landscapes more settled and broken of spirit.

ON A WARM APRIL MORNING, with a flood tide and a southwest breeze in our favor, we launch from near the little Nanticoke River town of Bivalve with a rasp of sand and oyster shells beneath our hulls. We are six men and three women, in seven single kayaks and one double. We chose kayaks for their speed, half again that of a canoe, for their ability to slither across a heavy dew, and for their stability—one's butt, the center of gravity, sits literally below the waterline. A spray skirt, extending down from the paddler's chest and snapping tightly over the rim of the cockpit, sheds waves and gives the whole affair the buoyancy of a cork. Able in high winds and seas, efficient enough to cover twenty miles a day and more, stealthy enough to sneak closer to wildlife than any other craft, the kayak is an instrument perfectly attuned to exploring the Chesapeake's mix of big, open water; shallow, intimate edges; and convoluted, intricate marsh-ways.

With favorable weather, we can do the trip in three days. We allow a fourth, anticipating at least three stretches where we will get temporarily lost or have trouble finding the six inches or so of water needed to float a kayak loaded with food and camping gear. Just as a substantial

Spartina alterniflora, *one of the bay's primary marsh grasses, requires regular tidal flooding.*

boat must have a name, so must a substantial expedition. Unlike a boat, an expedition's title need not fit a transom; so we propose this: The First Annual Trans-Dorchester Tribute to Sea-Level Rise Kayak Trip. It is a title that will lengthen as we progue farther into the Great Marsh—reaching some surprising and disturbing conclusions about this land where time only seems to stand still.

There's no dawdling on our first leg across the Nanticoke. It's the biggest open-water crossing we'll make, nearly two miles wide here, near its entry to Tangier Sound. Winds can quickly turn it rough and deadly to small craft. Also, while April days can be warm enough for T-shirt paddling, water temperatures remain cold enough to render an overturned boater helpless in a short time. All concerns drop away as our small band crosses successfully and enters the marshy embrace of Elliott's Island, easternmost of the peninsulas and island chains that dangle from the underbelly of lower Dorchester. In the shallows, wintering flocks of canvasbacks and bluebills are still feeding, fattening for migration north, even as ospreys, just arrived from as far south as Argentina, wheel overhead, spying out fish or driftwood sticks to build their nests.

The marsh vibrates with the spirited calling

of red-winged blackbirds, intent on staking out nesting areas. In a show of territoriality, male redwings cling to the swaying stems of reeds and cattails, displaying their brilliant shoulder patches. Against a blue sky, there is no more vivid or evocative portrait of spring in the Great Marsh. Occasional dark heads bob from the water and twist around to peer curiously at the kayaks as a flood tide boosts us westward through

a twisty little creek. The heads belong to diamondback terrapins, recently risen from winter burial in the mud of shallow coves. Some of the large old females have likely watched over these creeks for forty years or more.

From the thick banks of needlerush and cordgrass that wall us in, come the loud kek-kek-kek of clapper rails—like two dry sticks beaten smartly together. It would be hard to visit the

Winds accompanying a fall cold front whisk clouds and churn the waters of Tangier Sound as a group of kayakers head south along Bloodsworth Island.

A pair of wood ducks—male and female—glide through the early-morning fog on Chicone Creek.

14

Elliott marshes even once without hearing rails—there are several varieties—but you might come here for years and never see one, so secretive are they. Most elusive of all is the black rail, little larger than a sparrow. Bird-watchers for many years knew the marshes here were one of the best places in the country to hear black rails, but not one had ever seen one.

Brooke Meanley, a retired biologist, writes about a 1958 adventure, stalking Elliott's Island at night when the black rail is most active. Three men walked abreast, two holding lights and the one in the middle wielding a shotgun. Whenever a rail called, the light-holders triangulated, or crossed their beams on the spot, into which the middle man fired. Even such drastic techniques failed to produce so much as a feather. The first sighting of the rare bird occurred when Meanley heard one calling—from between his feet—and reached down and picked it up.

Now our well-defined creek-way through Elliott's has turned into the first real navigational test of the voyage, the passage devolving into a labyrinth of islands and shallow ponds, some with half a dozen outlets, only one of which will actually lead us on the way west across the Great Marsh. You could wander here all day. The lead paddler proceeds with the aid

of a series of high-altitude, color infrared photographs, laminated in plastic to waterproof them and strapped to the deck of his kayak. These were expensive, but the extreme detail and contrast they afford would prove the best way to avoid hours of exhausting trial and error.

Sixty years ago, this route wouldn't have been an option. Aerial photos of Elliott's Island taken in 1938 show mostly solid marsh where today's watery maze exists. Forces are at work in the Chesapeake that far exceed the foot-a-century rise in global sea level that has been going on for decades. A combination of subsiding lands and rising sea level is causing effective rates of rise as high as five feet a century in the last decade. To what extent this is caused by human activities, from global warming (sea-level rise) to pumping groundwater for farming and industry (land sinking), is still debated.

But humans have been changing this seemingly natural and changeless landscape in more ways than most people realize. Our aerial photos, for example, reveal an assortment of straight lines—striking against the natural meanders of the marsh. Decades of projects, public and private, to manipulate the marsh for mosquito control, for duck production, for muskrat trapping have left it scarred with ditches, impoundments,

The straight lines of man-made mosquito ditches contrast with the natural meanders of the marsh.

berms, canals, and water-control structures. On the whole, these have done more harm than good, interrupting natural processes in the marsh, compounding the stresses from sea-level rise.

With our fancy maps and a bit of luck, we make the Elliott's Island road by midmorning. It is our first and last portage—about thirty feet— the only time we will need to take our hulls out of the water in crossing the entire county. We'll intersect just two more roads before finishing the four-day journey, both at bridges.

I am no champion of roads, having grown up coincident with the first Chesapeake Bay Bridge that opened my native Eastern Shore to endless traffic; and even less a fan of extending more asphalt into the state's remaining remote environments. But the Elliott's Island road is special. A road in some form has existed here for close to three hundred years, its narrow track winding

A raccoon washes off his dinner at the water's edge.

A painted turtle catches some sun on a log in Big Creek.

some ten miles through open wetlands, bending around piney islands and skirting big, shallow tide ponds that mirror sky and marsh and turn every color of precious metals with the rising and setting sun.

The road to Elliott's has better nature viewing than the official Wildlife Drive that draws visitors from all over the world to nearby Blackwater National Wildlife Refuge. Where it first emerges onto the Great Marsh, the water is fresh, and tall cattails and lavish pink and cream hibiscus flowers line the road's edges. Further on, a bit soggier, a bit saltier, meadows of *Spartina patens*, salt-marsh hay, grow as dense

and lush as the fur on an animal's pelt, remaining emerald green through the droughtiest summers. Vast stands of needlerush fall away to the horizons, changing color and texture with every passing mood of the day and the breeze. Some days, as the rising sun streams through the rushes, dragonflies cling to every stalk, their wings sparkling like jewels as far as one can see.

Within fifty yards of the road, bald eagles perch atop muskrat lodges. Egrets and herons, ibis and stilts, every manner of elegant wading bird, strut across the mirror-like surfaces of the tide ponds. Possums, coons, sikas, and white-tailed deer, also muskrats, nutria, marsh hawks,

A Delmarva fox squirrel chews on the stalk of a plant at Blackwater Refuge. This squirrel is on the endangered species list.

and waterfowl from tundra swans to quick-winged little teal—all carry on their business as if the road was not there.

One weekday evening I hiked the road for two hours before I met a vehicle. But it was no silent place—racketing, twanging, barooming, peeping frogs, in dizzying variety, saw to that, as did great horned and barred owls, barking foxes, bugling sikas (actually a miniature species of elk), and the ever-present legions of rails. On rain-soaked nights, the little roadway is clogged with the traffic of frogs; and by day, in nesting season, it is one long terrapin crossing.

There are no finer vistas available to Maryland motorists than the Elliott's Island road for watching an advancing cold front, or a thunderstorm, pass across the Great Marsh, their comings and goings visible for miles. The everyday play of the elements on the tableaux of marsh there recalls Marjory Stoneman Douglas's

A pair of fox cubs stare curiously at a camouflaged photographer as he creeps toward them on a farm lane.

20 classic *River of Grass*, describing the Everglades: "Their vast glittering openness, wider than the enormous visible round of the horizon, the racing free saltness and sweetness of their massive winds, under the dazzling blue heights of space, the miracle of the light pours over the green and brown expanse." All the above is best seen from the safety of a vehicle, for hungry mosquitoes are the most common wildlife along the Elliott's Island road, thick enough to cloud a camera lens on windless days.

WE'VE MADE OUR PORTAGE by 10.30 a.m. I fear we have allowed too much time for the trip. From the road we can see forested Guinea Island, our destination the first night—have been able to see it since we left, in fact, and will see it behind us for nearly two days after we leave it. Lower Dorchester is that flat and open. But what looks near in the Great Marsh often isn't

A winter morning is reflected in the tidal ponds along the edge of Chance Island, a rare outpost of high ground along the lower Transquaking River.

so easily reached. The town of Elliott, for example, is only five miles across Fishing Bay from Bishops Head, a community on the next long peninsula to the west. Yet the road connecting them, which must follow the high ground, stretches fifty miles. And from Bishops Head to Hoopersville, the next appendage of land heading west, the story is the same. At the dawn of the twenty-first century, a kayak can still be as quick as a car in making connections down here.

Indeed, after the next hour and a half of hard paddling, Guinea Island seems not much closer. The flood tide from the Nanticoke, which boosted us for a while, is surging against us from the Fishing Bay side of Elliott's. Through an interminable series of bends, the water's force is sufficient to thrust the kayaks sideways every time a corner is rounded. With relief, we emerge onto Fishing Bay, a broad body of water

Waves punch incessantly at the edges of the Great Marsh. The sea-level rise and the subsidence of the land compound the erosion that has taken thousands of acres in recent decades.

Chunks of ice thrown up by a passing outboard catch the morning sun to create the illusion of glowing embers on a frozen gut through Bloodsworth Island.

covering some thirty square miles. This could be one nasty paddle in the right wind. Its shallow waters make up a sharp, steep chop in minutes. This day it's so flat that the workboats of early spring crabbers plying their trotlines seem suspended in a monochrome merge of sky and sea. From a distance, they move to and fro soundlessly, shimmering in the noonday heat coming off the marsh and the water. It is a timeless Chesapeake scene, and one can imagine Native Americans, centuries earlier, harvesting the bay's seafood from dugout canoes, in methods not that far removed from those of today's watermen.

marsh, with a narrow river (the Transquaking) cutting through it. Stevenson theorizes that a mammoth East Coast storm—one is documented in 1827—could have backed water up in the marshes here for days, long enough to begin a terminal process of decomposition of the underlying peat layers. It is the same process he has documented happening today in the Great Marsh, on a slower time scale, from sea-level rise. The influence even one storm can have in a place as low-lying as the Great Marsh was apparent after the big hurricane of August 1933. The saltwater flooding caused by the August storm was enough to close down most of the small but thriving vegetable-growing industry in Dorchester County. The land, untilled, reverted to pine forest and marsh.

Following the eastern shoreline of Fishing Bay, we finally reach the mouth of the Transquaking and the lower end of Guinea Island. We've been on the water for some two and a half

In fact, such a scene probably never occurred here. Fishing Bay apparently never existed until a great storm blew through these parts some 180 years ago. J. Court Stevenson, a University of Maryland marine ecologist who has studied the Dorchester marshes, has examined all the old maps of the Chesapeake in the state archives; and before the 1820s, he cannot find Fishing Bay depicted, only what appears to be a low

Pinkish early-morning light and "slick cam" conditions accent Elihu Abbott's workboat, Cat Fish, *as he heads out for a morning of crabbing.*

hours without encountering a square foot of land high and dry enough to make a good rest stop. It's a mere taste of what's to come the next day, when we will add another theme to the title of our expedition: The Search for High Ground. That evening, though, for the only time in the trip, we have a surplus of dry land. State-owned Guinea Island is an anomaly, a forested tract of nearly a square mile, rising up to twelve feet above sea level, surrounded on every side by the state's greatest expanse of wetlands. We make camp beneath oak trees, on a sandy bluff above the Transquaking where the shadbush is blooming in white, frothy splendor.

Information about Guinea is scarce. There was never a European settlement here, though the foundation of a home still peeks through the undergrowth in an old clearing now regrowing in saplings. It must have been a prime encampment for the Indians, bounded by a navigable

Elihu Abbott traces his lineage back to the earliest inhabitants of the Great Marsh, long before contact with European settlers.

28

Years of plunging his hands into ice-cold water to set and remove muskrat traps have taken their toll on Elihu Abbott. His arthritic hands steer his boat by push-ing and pulling the tiller stick to make it go left and right.

river whose current bore great spring spawning runs of herring, shad, and striped bass and surrounded by a marsh rich in muskrat, otter, and all manner of waterfowl. Elihu Abbott, a retired fur trapper who traces his lineage in the Great Marsh back to Native Americans, comes to camp on Guinea with his family each year. The forest there today, impressive to us, "is nothin' but sprigs" compared to the stands of virgin pine he knew there as a young man. A sawmill was established during World War II to take out the big trees, which "were so big it would take two of me [his arms stretched wide] to get around one."

Abbott at 71 still has coal-black hair, accentuating high cheekbones in a brown, angular face. His hands are gnarled now, arthritic from too many years of plunging into freezing water for "rats" caught in his traps; but in his prime, he was the fastest muskrat skinner anyone had

Net ready, Elihu Abbott slowly works his way along a trotline, looking for crabs in the Honga River. Pieces of eel or chicken necks are tied along the line at regular intervals to attract the tasty crabs, which come into view as the line moves across a roller attached to the boat.

ever seen. The *Baltimore Sun* recounts the record he set in 1955 in a national contest: "The crowd gasped and burst into applause when, with a rebel yell, he tossed his third pelt to the floor after less than 50 seconds." In 1959 he very nearly became the first and only man to skin five rats in less than a minute (one of the timers that the judges used caught him a bit under, the other a bit over). Guinea, which he can see from atop his house, a day's paddle distant, was renowned for growing more than big trees, he says.

"It always was a good place to find arrow-heads, and fertile? That soil'd grow anything, melons so big you'd need a mule to get 'em out. And the squirrels that used to live out there. No one ever saw anything like it. They were those big fox squirrels [an endangered species depen-dent on old-growth forests] near two and a half feet long. And there were no two alike—white ears, heads black as smut, grays, colors all

A "sook," a mature female crab in the final stage of its life, clings to a dip net. The "Capitol dome" shape on the underside of its shell identifies it.

A blue crab is caught in Elihu Abbott's net as he trotlines in the Honga River.

mixed. I guess they had inbred so much they were crazy colored. I haven't seen a squirrel there in fifteen years now."

From Guinea, which we have been looking at most of the day, we can look back and see the buildings on the Nanticoke's eastern shore where we began. Before dinner, the bay gives us a healthy taste of how changeable it can be in April. Some of us were about to dig bathing suits out of our dry bags to cool off from the warm afternoon's paddle. Minutes later, an approaching thunderstorm had me digging through my bag for long underwear and rain gear. For the next two hours, the Great Marsh crackled and boomed and flashed. The wind drove rain horizontally across our campsite and whipped the fire to such a frenzy it was consuming a log, it seemed, every few minutes.

Not much to show for a morning's work, crabs line the bottom of a bushel basket. Abbott has seen his catch diminish over the years. He crabs now mostly for his own dinner table.

The glow of lightning and the green trails of lightning bugs in a time exposure illuminate a marsh near Bishops Head.

Some of us took to the tents, but others stayed on the bluff to watch the show. As the storm raged, Scott, who is six feet eight inches tall, extended his arms wide, turned into the driving rain, and roared at the thunder and lightning: "This is just sooo. . . PERFECT!!!"

DAY TWO BREAKS SUNNY, in the low 70s, light breeze. A good day to die, remarks someone with little faith in our aerial maps. We'll need them, because the route is going to be Elliott's Island times three in its complexity—a marshy maze, wild country, through places with names like Wolfpit and Beargarden (Backgarden on modern maps). But the best maps money can buy prove to be worth every penny. After a few hours we make it through, picking up the main channel of the Blackwater River. We've calculated on a strong tide pushing us upriver, into the National Wildlife Refuge. Only a very

strong paddler would want to fight the current in the Blackwater for long. A stiff breeze is at our backs, too—and then it is in our faces, then behind us, then . . . You can't win in the twisty Blackwater, which curves and toils back upon itself like few other Chesapeake waterways.

Sometimes the loopbacks are so extreme that the lead kayaks and those last in line, though half a mile apart as the river flows, pass within twenty yards of one another. If yesterday was The Search for High Ground, today has become The Search for Any Ground. Bathroom breaks on the marsh, ankle-to-knee deep in cold water, are an experience, especially for the ladies. One's kayak spray skirts afford the only privacy.

A few watermen in skiffs are working the river channel today, baiting long, cylindrical

OPPOSITE: *David Lieben-berg explores an old dock on the upper Blackwater River.*

Ed Dryden paddles along Coles Creek on a still spring morning.

wire "pots," or traps for eels, one of the first types of fishing to awaken in the Chesapeake spring. Many visitors know the Great Marsh for its more visible migrations of warblers and ospreys arriving each spring, and for the legions of waterfowl that flock there in fall. Few are aware how the lowly eel, after years of residence in the muds of rivers like the Blackwater, under-goes an autumn transformation, adding fat and taking on a silver sheen before setting off on moonless nights to join other eels from across North America in the Sargasso Sea. Spawning there at depths so great that their reproduction has never been witnessed, the adult eels all die. Somehow their young, transported by cur-rents and guided by mysterious senses, repopu-late every waterway to their smallest headwater streams.

Spring is also stirring greenly along large portions of our route in tender shoots of bul-rush, or scirpus, pushing up through the charred stubble of last year's marsh. Charred because vast acreages of this landscape where nature seems still to dominate are in fact rou-tinely manipulated by human-set fires for a single, somewhat controversial, purpose. Had we been kayaking the Great Marsh a couple months earlier, we would have witnessed it blossoming with scattered eruptions of deep orange from the burning, billows of smoke, turning from black to whitish-gray wherever the flames encountered pines and other islands of upland vegetation (the thick-barked pines usually survive, though wind-whipped flames sometimes destroy them).

"Around the start of burning season [January 1] the calls come two or three a night—'burn me first,' 'burn me,' 'burn me soon,'" says Bill Geise, a federal employee at the Blackwater National

Wildlife Refuge who has a lifelong, intimate relationship with the Great Marsh. The calls are from fur trappers—mostly after muskrat—all wanting the acreage they trap put to the torch. The burning does two things, Geise says. It arrests the normal succession of the marsh to upland, woody vegetation, favoring the pioneering, emergent scirpus, which is manna to muskrats. It also makes the marshes eminently walkable, and accessible to trappers. Each spring Blackwater, which leases trapping rights to its marsh, burns some three thousand acres. The state of Maryland and private owners burn perhaps another six thousand.

The peaty, humusy soils that underlie a lot of the Great Marsh make it some of the best scirpus habitat anywhere. The same soils also lend themselves to muskrats, perfect for their tunneling. For a while, back in the 1920s and '30s, this combined with a robust world fur mar-

A tricolor heron carefully walks the shallows in search of dinner.

ket to make Dorchester wetlands worth more than good farmland. Muskrat pelts sold for as high as four dollars, a relative fortune then, and by 1938 trappers were taking close to a quarter-million hides a year out of the Great Marsh. Delmarva Fur Farms, a now-forgotten commercial venture, employed teams of trappers to work the marshes round the clock, Geise says. Its owners invented a special trap that, when a muskrat tripped it, would send a flag up to signal waiting trappers. At night, tripping a trap sent off a carbide flare. Throughout the Great Marsh, old ditches, water impoundments, even major canals dug to shortcut the looping chan-

nels of rivers—all testify to human modification in the name of the fur trade.

In modern times, both the demand for fur and the numbers of muskrats have dropped considerably. Probably no more than a few dozen local men, women, and school kids seriously trap the Great Marsh, and even for those, "a hobby is about all it amounts to . . . trapping's a dying thing," says Geise, who is himself a trapper.

But the tradition runs strong. Geise notes that "many a kid down here's gone through college on rats; rats have gotten many a family through the winter." On a February weekend,

A lesser yellowlegs forages in the mudflats of Island Creek at low tide.

close to a thousand people pack into the South Dorchester elementary and middle school at Golden Hill for the National Outdoor Show, held since 1938. It features quilting, fishnet weaving, carving, wild-game cooking; also contests in fur skinning, duck and goose calling, pole skinning (the poles used to set fish pounds, or traps, each spring), trap setting, and crosscut sawing. It is remarkable that, with the sole exception of crosscut sawing, every skill on display is still in active use across the Great Marsh.

WE'VE BEEN ON THE WATER four hours when the Maple Dam Road bridge over the Black- water at Shorter's Wharf comes in sight—the first road since Elliott's Island. A small community of weathered homes, mostly vacant, clings to a couple acres of dry land around the bridge. An hour later, we're still watching the bridge swing into view and fall away behind us. Such is the loopy nature of the Blackwater. Reaching Shorter's Wharf is a joyful occasion, because we've stashed bushels of oysters and clams, and cold beer, in a truck we parked there two days ago. The first breakdown of the trip has occurred—the welded aluminum rudder of one kayak has sheared off. One of our band knows a boatbuilder over in Wingate, fifteen miles away,

Tundra swans catch the dying rays of a late winter sunset over Wolfpit Marsh, part of the Blackwater National Wildlife Refuge. In a few weeks, they will migrate north to their breeding grounds in the Arctic regions.

and goes off in the truck. In two hours he is back with a beautiful repair that we probably couldn't have obtained had we been in Baltimore Harbor.

We had thought to camp at Shorter's, but except for a small cemetery, even the highest ground is soggy. So, balancing oysters and beer on the decks of our slender craft, we paddle an hour out of the way to Barnes Landing, a little-used local launching spot at the end of a long, rutted dirt road. The landing, baking under a 2 P.M. sun, is little more than a few square yards of hard, hot, lumpy clay. The only place high enough to crowd our tents on is a ditch bank some two hundred yards up the road. Even that is none too level, with bare earth so hard-baked you can't drive a tent stake into it. All around is fresh-burned marsh, which grimes our gear with charcoal.

OPPOSITE: *A time exposure on a starry night captures the rotation of the earth and light from a campfire reflected in the pines at Barnes Landing.*

A nutria scurries through stubble of a recently burned marsh. These South American beavers have spread throughout the marsh, outcompeting native muskrats and destroying vegetation.

Near evening, the falling light begins to cool and soften our surroundings. As we look back over where we have come from, the setting sun kindles a tawny, golden light across a sea of marsh that fairly glows before fading. You can still see Guinea, a blue-green smudge on the horizon; and as dark comes on, the lights of Elliott twinkle. At full dark, a few lights come up back on the Wicomico shore of the Nanticoke, two full days behind us. Only two roads bisect all that emptiness. An hour passes, during which we see only one set of headlights moving across either one.

As we stargaze in the delicious cool of the night, the comet Hale-Bopp emerges, so bright you can see the full, majestic spread of its fiery tail. The night music of the Great Marsh pipes up—owls hoot, Canada geese honk, and all around are the truncated wails of nutria, South American beavers that were imported decades ago and have spread throughout the bay's wetlands.

AROUND DAWN, a few of us paddle further up the creek that flows by Barnes Landing. Textures and colors of forest and marsh reflect prettily on its slatey calm surface. It's a veritable nutria highway. Literally dozens of the fifteen-to-twenty-pound rodents are swimming the creek or lounging along its banks. They act like they own the place, and perhaps they do.

The morning soon turns showery and gray. A sou'easter has blown in off the Atlantic Ocean. Fortunately, the wind will be at our backs most of the day. We'll be passing through the heart of the sprawling, 25,500-acre Blackwater National Wildlife Refuge, whose rules set our schedule for this voyage. You can't paddle through before the migrating waterfowl leave in April, or after they begin returning in September. Given the

A bald eagle protects his dinner of nutria left on a marsh bank by a trapper, who needed only to turn in the rodent's tail to qualify for a bounty payment.

bugginess of summertime, that leaves narrow windows for a through passage.

Even the cold rain can't dampen our spirits. We've seen close to a dozen magnificent bald eagles in the first hour on the water, outnumbering all the humans we will meet in the four-day journey. It is good to see them coming back from the brink of extinction, victimized by now-banned pesticides like DDT. They are raptors,

a word that shares the same Latin root with *rapture*—and no wonder, for the sight of their soaring seizes the spirit, lofts the soul. Never mind that they relish carrion as well as fresh fish and will just as soon bully smaller birds out of their prey as work for it themselves. Soaring high, wide, and handsome, opportunistic and greedy; big, good-looking dudes, comeback kids, a bit of the bully—all in all, they are a most fitting national symbol.

In all the Chesapeake region, the refuge and the Great Marsh best provided the essentials for *Haliaeetus leucocephalus*'s stirring comeback— solitude, a healthy supply of fish and game, and an abundance of land-water edge. A survey of 367 historic bald eagle nests in Maryland and Virginia showed that 95 percent were less than two miles from open water, and 60 percent were less than half a mile. Eagles do almost all of their feeding within a hundred yards of shorelines and spend 90 percent of their time perching, usually on tall trees within sight of water's edge. In the summer one can see their young learning to fish by gliding from such perch trees to the water. So it is not surprising, in this landscape where water and land intertwine, that Dorchester held about a fourth of the 835 bald eagles surveyed in the year 2000 throughout

A mature bald eagle fends off younger members of his species to protect his dinner of nutria entrails left by a trapper. Young bald eagles don't get distinctive white feathers on head and tail until they are a few years old.

Maryland's twenty-three counties. Only thirty
years before, in July 1970, the news that a single
eaglet had hatched at Blackwater—the first
since 1955—made headlines in the *Baltimore
Sun.*

When you paddle a kayak hour after hour,
the rhythmic push-pull of stroking with the
double-bladed paddle becomes almost medita-
tive. The scenery today—classic lower Dorchester—encourages that: endless vistas of water and
salt marsh, punctuated by islands of tall, skinny
loblolly pine. The islands have whimsical names
like Barbados and Cole Comfort. Soon, the
banks of the Blackwater begin to gap, then fall
away entirely, leaving us to navigate across a vast
lake.

Because it bears so little sign of human de-
velopment, it is easy to describe the refuge as
"timeless." But as recently as the late 1950s, the
river here still wound through marshes of tall

cordgrass as far as the Route 335 bridge, still an hour's paddle ahead. Aerial photographs have confirmed that as much as seven thousand acres, about ten square miles of marsh, have turned to open water in the refuge since the 1930s.

This dissolving marsh creates some of the most difficult paddling of the trip. You can run aground on a barely submerged lump of peat, try to step out of the kayak to push off, and hit holes several feet deep. Nothing marks the channel except a few osprey nests that refuge workers have erected on poles to guide their skiffs, but these are too far apart to help anyone who does not run the route frequently.

The major culprit appears to be the rising sea level, says Court Stevenson, who has studied the Blackwater area intensively. Just a small change in the water level can make all the difference. Experiments that pumped sediment up to

raise disappearing marshes in the refuge brought dramatic comebacks in wetland vegetation when just four inches of elevation were added. Up and down the roads of lower Dorchester County you can see people's attempts to cope—driveways humped up a foot or two to park cars during high tides, yards diked with earthen berms, and grassy mounds behind homes where piling up sand is the only way to percolate and filter septic-tank wastes in otherwise soggy soils.

Stevenson also notes that not all marshes are created equal. Some get a goodly supply of sediment flowing down rivers, or across barrier is-

Mud is the literal bottom line in much of Dorchester County. Its grasp makes a long walk out of a short distance in the marsh.

*High tide from the Black-
water River frequently
covers Maple Dam Road at
Shorter's Wharf.*

lands, which enables them to build elevation faster than the sea level is rising; but it is not so in much of Dorchester County. The marshes here have only their own decaying organic matter to build on. The crumbly peat base dissolves all too easily when water covers it for too long. That may be why the huge storm in the 1820s, backing up tide upon tide, was able to carve out Fishing Bay so quickly. Ironically, it is this soft, peaty quality of the Great Marsh, perfect for tunneling by muskrats and good growing for scirpus, that has made it such a fur factory.

As if the stress of a rising sea level wasn't enough to contend with, the Great Marsh has come under assault from inhabitants that scarcely existed a few decades ago. The Canada goose music we've gone to sleep by these last two nights is, of course, considered as synonymous with the Eastern Shore as crab feasts and oysters—but here in April, it is past time

for Canada geese to be back north in Labrador, busily about their nesting. These geese, however, are a western subspecies of Canada, introduced to the East Coast decades ago, and never will migrate. Their numbers have built from a few thousand to a million or more now, outnumbering their migratory cousins.

Paddling through the refuge today, we have noticed them nesting on every available spot of high marsh. The refuge has some six thousand now, up from five hundred a decade or so ago. Across the Eastern Shore they are becoming nuisances, "greasing" lawns and golf courses with their feces and closing swimming ponds and lakes with bacterial pollution when the weather heats up. Emergent marsh vegetation is choice food for the "resident" geese, as they are called. Another species, the lesser snow goose, has also been expanding its population dramatically. While the snows are migratory, their feeding habits make

them "some of the worst marsh killers there are," says Blackwater's Bill Geise.

Then there are the nutria. With their orange buck teeth, the misnamed creatures (*nutria* is Spanish for *otter*) resemble giant, coarse-haired guinea pigs. Originally imported to Louisiana in the 1930s, they escaped, or were released, and have spread into forty states now. Trappers and biologists say they love the same

scirpus reeds as muskrats; but unlike muskrats, which graze on it, nutria consume the roots and all. On our route, we see patches of nutria-infested marsh that appear chewed literally to the nub, little more than a mudflat.

A brief fur market that encouraged nutria trapping has disappeared, and while a local meat market for muskrats flourishes, no one wants to

eat nutria. Some of us have tried both and think nutria meat lighter and less gamey, but local tastes are hard to change. There is talk of an eradication campaign against the nutria, and studies are under way to determine whether it could succeed; but few think it could. Meanwhile, numbers of native muskrats have been dropping. Last year the Elliott's Island United Methodist Church had to postpone its annual February muskrat dinner for a month to get enough of the critters to feed a crowd; and the town of Bivalve suffered the ignominy of having to import muskrats from Ohio for its annual fest.

Most controversial is the damage to wetlands from frequently firing the Great Marsh to sustain trapping. Ecologist Court Stevenson thinks it is destroying vegetation that could be helping to form new peat to stay ahead of the sea-level rise; it also favors the predations of nutria and resident geese by maintaining the kind of open marsh that makes ideal habitat and food for them (without burning, most marshes would revert to shrubs and other, more upland vegetation). "It's like putting out ice cream for nutria and geese," he says. "We're managing for a few species instead of a healthy ecosystem." Politically, any suggestion that burning be stopped is

A family of Canada geese cross Maple Dam Road in an increasingly familiar summer scene around Chesapeake Bay. The increase in resident Canada geese has alarmed wildlife managers.

ABOVE: *Under Mom's watchful eye, a group of mute swan cygnets sun themselves on a Hooper Island beach. A European import, mute swans have become a threat to native birds' nesting areas and are consuming underwater grasses that serve as valuable habitat for crabs and fish.*

A mute swan family enjoy an outing on a spring afternoon.

OPPOSITE: *New green growth of the phragmites reed will eventually reach the height of the brown tassels from last year's plants. The reed appears to be spreading in bay marshes, crowding out plants of greater wildlife value.*

a hot potato. A blue-ribbon science panel that evaluated it a few years ago essentially called for more evaluation.

At any rate, what we've seen in the last day suggests adding to the already lengthy theme of the trip yet another: The Ever-Changing Nature of a Natural Landscape.

Now it's afternoon of our third day, and the landscape is undergoing its most profound change since we first shoved off from the Wicomico shore of the Nanticoke. After a slog across the inland marsh-loss sea, we've passed under the Route 335 bridge, the road to Hoopers Island, taking on our last cache of food and beverage. The Blackwater regains its de-fined channel, and something else is happening: the water, dark and turbid all day, is becoming a pure, translucent black. From the depths, the sinuous, wine-red stems of lily pads rise. In a

. . . and perhaps even slower going for an outboard.

couple months, most of the river will be covered with these, opening their creamy, goblet-shaped blossoms to the morning sun. The river, from a distance, will look some mornings like a cotton field when the bolls burst open.

The lilies are a sign that we've finally escaped the Chesapeake's salty influence, and a stop to check a fish trap set in the river confirms it—the net is loaded with crappie and bluegills, both freshwater species. The forest begins to reassert itself on the banks. Rounding one bend, we pass directly under a giant nest with two eaglets in it. With light failing and a campsite near, we make a brief excursion into a shallow, mucky cove, leaving our kayaks to join hands and trudge, thigh-deep in clinging, black mud. It's not long before our human chain strikes the rare find Bill

A log canoe, most likely built by European settlers in the colonial period, lies partially submerged along the Black-water River after being carefully removed from its resting place in the river by a state archaeologist. This canoe can help archaeologists understand how the design and construction of the log canoe evolved from those used by native peoples to those adopted by colonial settlers.

Geise told us had been concealed here for centuries.

Geise was setting nest boxes in the cove for wood ducks some years back, and every time he would motor in to the shore in his skiff, his propeller would strike a submerged log. One day, when the water was unusually clear, he thought he'd have a look at that log, with an eye to hauling it out of the way. It turned out to be the well-preserved hull of a dugout canoe, hewn from a single great log, some twelve feet in length and a couple feet in the beam. A later visit with an archaeologist determined that it was not of Indian construction, but made with a colonial technique.

Early colonists would drill holes in a log to the depth they wanted for the thickness of the canoe's bottom, and insert pegs. Hollowing the log out from the inside, when they hit the pegs, they knew they had reached the desired bottom thickness. Someday the canoe may be salvaged and preserved. Until then, its ancient wood is best protected by leaving it in the Blackwater's bottom.

Archaeologist Bruce Thompson settles in the muck of the Blackwater River to measure a historical-period log canoe he and a team of volunteers retrieved from the river's bottom. Though the earlier canoes used by native peoples were made with the use of fire, this one will help show how design and construction methods changed as the colonials used metal tools to hollow out the logs.

THE THIRD NIGHT'S CAMPSITE on the upper Blackwater is the prettiest yet, a peninsula of tall pines, oak, and sweetgum. It's the first return to high ground since Guinea Island. Level and carpeted with soft pine needles, with big fallen logs to lean one's back against, it's a fine vantage point from which to once again look back. Guinea Island was still visible until the last few turns in the river. We've come almost from Nanticoke to Choptank, from oyster grounds and salt marsh to bluegills and lily-pads; three days and two nights and almost no lights, no houses, and no traffic. It's a certainty that not a yard of our route hasn't many times seen the keel of someone else's boat—trapper, fisherman, deer hunter, wildlife manager— but the whole of the passage, an extraordinary transect through the heart of the Great Marsh, is greater than the sum of its parts.

LAST DAY, THE FINAL PUSH, spirits are high. We're close to our goal, or so it looks from the maps. The river narrows through ranks of forest. Pines on one side are obviously dying, victims, we suspect, of the sea-level rise. Now we are paddling single file as the Blackwater narrows to a stream. Then it becomes lost in a jumble of channels splaying off through marsh and forest. The water by now has changed again, from fresh and dark to grayish and salty. We are getting flow from the Little Choptank.

This is the break in the watersheds, where the land between the rivers is dissolving. Even

A bullfrog peeks above the algae-choked surface of a pond near Shorter's Wharf

Their black-tipped wings and white bodies highlighted by the winter sun, a flock of snow geese fly over farm fields.

with the aerial photos, we begin making wrong turns. It's raining heavily now. The deteriorating marsh here is a hodgepodge of tumps and holes, even worse paddling than the day before, on the refuge's inland sea. You can't paddle and you can't get out and walk. All you can do is dig at the muck and shove along. At one point, some of us in the heavier-loaded kayaks have to plant our hands to each side and strain to raise our own weight and that of the boat enough to inch forward.

We follow until the lead boat runs aground, then split to either side until someone else runs aground or finds a channel. It's slow and agonizing work. A hunter standing on one bank calls to us: "That doesn't go through, you know." Indeed, had the wind been northwest, a direction that usually lowers water levels in the Chesapeake, we would have had to turn back. But then, after covering perhaps half a mile in an hour, we are through, cruising across a broad pond that reflects the stormy sky with a lovely, silvery-gray sheen. A short paddle brings us to an old canal, originally cut to take logs out of the forests here, and soon we have passed under the Taylor's Island road and heard once again the crunch of sand and shell beneath the kayaks on the Little Choptank's shore.

As the crow flies, we have come perhaps twenty-five miles, but we've paddled more than twice that as the Great Marsh dictates things. In the short run, the break between the watersheds

The full moon rises behind a copse of pine trees near Bishops Head. Increased salinity due to the rising sea level is killing trees in what formerly were high spots in the marsh.

With their paddles in perfect sync, a group of kayakers head across Hooper Straits for an early-morning outing. The Deal Island bridge can be seen in the distance.

will only get easier to traverse, and in the long run, the sea-level rise may turn large sections of our route into open water. In the meantime, refuge officials are negotiating with the Army Corps of Engineers to use sediments dredged from bay channels to rebuild the marsh and block saltwater intrusions that further endanger many rare plants of the upper Blackwater's unique freshwater ecosystem.

We wish them success, happy that we, like the wildlife of the Great Marsh, have seized the day, made the best of changing conditions, and completed the First Annual Trans-Dorchester Tribute to Sea-Level Rise, Search for High Ground, and Ever-Changing Nature of a Natural Landscape Kayak Trip.

*Needlerush and the full moon
are reflected in the water
at the edge of a marsh in the
Blackwater National Wild-
life Refuge.*

A cap of snow on an over-turned bushel basket makes it stand out in the winter marsh. Although this basket will most likely decompose over a relatively brief time, wood is being replaced by plastic baskets, which will take many generations to decompose.

The first full moon of the year sets just before sunrise on a bitter cold morning at Bishops Head.

A light snow sugarcoats loblolly pine trees and panic grasses at the edge of a forest in the Kuehnle area of Blackwater National Wildlife Refuge.

A pair of American bald eagles sit on their nest atop a loblolly pine tree on a cold, snowy February morning. Nearly wiped out by the effects of the pesticide DDT a few decades ago, the popu-

lation of eagles has flourished lately, and the bald eagle was removed from the endangered species list in 1999.

Straight lines are rare in the Great Marsh. An icy road near Bestpitch Ferry seems to stretch to the horizon.

A yellow-rumped warbler scratches for a meal in the snow.

Streaks of light from the setting sun wash over a road at Wolfpit Creek. The road is used by trappers to gain access to muskrat traps inside Blackwater National Wildlife Refuge.

*A wing print—most likely
from a great horned owl—
probably points to the
capture of a mouse or other
rodent from a snowbank at
the edge of Hooper Straits.*

TRAPPING

Sunset's pale afterglow rims the Great Marsh with cold, red light one February evening as we turn down an unmarked dirt drive that ends by a windowless shed. Only a few pickup trucks parked outside hint that anyone is there.

The door opens, releasing a flood of light and warmth and laughter, and the pungence of freshly skinned and gutted animals. Inside Robby Willey's fur shed, it's a family affair. His 6-year-old, Samantha, sweeps scraps of flesh and fur from the concrete floor, piling them in a wheelbarrow. Robby's wife, Anne; his dad, Guy; and Buck, a nephew, all are engaged in skinning, fleshing, stretching, and drying—the various stages of turning piles of muskrats into marketable pelts.

A few quick cuts of the skinning knife and a tug or two divests each muskrat of its hide—a good skinner can do one in half a minute or less. Turned inside out, the fresh, pliable "rat" hide is secured over a V-shaped board and scraped of any remaining flesh with a curved blade, grasped by handles on both ends.

Robby leans into his work, talking as he fleshes. He's 36, has been trapping since he was 8, and this is the first year there hasn't been a local fur buyer anywhere in Dorchester County. Worldwide, the demand for fur is down. There are probably no more than a dozen serious trappers left on the Great Marsh, and most of those, he says, are just doing it to supply the traditional local demand for meat. A coon fetches around three bucks, a muskrat two. As for nutria, the imported South American cousin of the beaver that has become a pest here, damaging the marsh, "I sold about forty to fifty for two dollars apiece, just trying to establish some kind of meat market. People said they liked 'em.

"It may sound dumb, but I'm doing this as kind of a hobby, even if I never sell my furs. It's

Laden with muskrats, Robby Willey walks his trapline in Wolfpit Marsh. The pole he carries marks the location of a trap. Note the arm-length trapper's glove to protect him from the freezing water.

a chance to stay outside and look around and stay in shape." Robby's main income is from vegetable farming. Anne works at a marine research laboratory, and Guy is retired from Blackwater National Wildlife Refuge. The shed, no more than 25 by 35 feet, seems even more crowded because of the unsold pelts that hang from rafters everywhere—a hundred foxes, two hundred muskrats, a dozen possums, and some two thousand nutria.

In the 1930s, Guy Willey chimes in, marsh here was more valuable than farmland. "A black rat [a color variation on the normal brown, for which the marshes here were famous] was four bucks, and gas was ten cents and Coke five cents. Now, a black rat gets you less than that, and you know what gas and Coke have done."

The door opens. It's Ronnie Robbins, a trapper from Hoopers Island. He shucks off his overcoat and joins in. He and Robby are

*Clad in hip waders and cam-
ouflage, Samantha Willey
accompanies her father,
Robby, as he checks muskrat
traps in Wolfpit Marsh.*

A muskrat dines on roadside grasses along the Wildlife Drive at Blackwater Refuge.

friendly competitors, keeping a weekly tally of how each is doing. Robby won last week, with 196 rats to Ronnie's 134; but for the month, Ronnie's up by 6, he says.

The two stayed at the fur shed late the night before, honing their skills for the fierce competitions at the upcoming National Outdoor Show. It started from a winter picnic organized in 1936 by farmers around the Great Marsh, who held a muskrat-skinning contest. The show has been held every winter since 1938, except for a few years during World War II.

Ronnie says each contestant chooses his own rats. He likes "a medium-big-sized one" because of his large hands. He is a former world champion who has skinned three rats in 45 seconds. Last night, practicing, he did a rat in 18 seconds; also, practicing for the trap-setting contest, he set six in 15 seconds. While his elders talk, Buck practices setting traps for the show's junior competitions.

Robby, whose skinning looks lightning fast, says he's not quick enough on rats to enter the show—"You need to be able to do five in less than two minutes to even be competitive. But I'm pretty quick on coons." Last year, three minutes for a single coon took top honors at the show, and Robby in practice has done one in 58 seconds. He's been keeping a live coon at home, "feeding him nothing but carrots, to tighten 'im up, make him skin out faster."

As we leave for home, driving across the dark, moonless marsh, the fur shed is still in full swing. "See you at the show," Robby says.

Indeed, that next weekend we see what seems like most of lower Dorchester County, several hundred people packed into the gym of the old South Dorchester High School at

Robby Willey, with nutria,
muskrat, and fox pelts
and the tools of the trapping
and skinning trade.

Golden Hill. Crab cakes, oyster fritters, crab soup, and oyster stew highlight the menu. Duck and goose callers vie for prizes and warm up the crowd for the skinning contests. The best callers manage to sound like a whole flock of waterfowl.

In the junior trap-setting, Buck is going great, arming the delicate trigger mechanism of trap after trap, lining them up on a table. But then one trips, and it unnerves the youth. You can see his hands tremble, and he trips another, and another, finishing behind another boy.

Ronnie acquits himself well in the men's muskrat skinning, but no one is a match for the lightning hands of Wylie Abbott, Jr., who finishes a whole rat ahead of his nearest competitor. He or his father, Wylie Abbott, Sr., have won the championship twenty-two times since 1970.

Coon-skinning has been made a special dem-

Samantha Willey waits in her father's pickup truck as he heads off to check his traps in the Blackwater National Wildlife Refuge.

onstration tonight. It will be just Robby and the carrot coon in a race against the clock. Accompanied by the 6-year-old Sam, he pulls one end of a volleyball net from behind the stage curtains and strings Carrot Coon from the pole by one hind leg. Following several quick cuts with the skinning knife, Sam slaps a special tool into Robby's hand, like a practiced surgical nurse in the O.R. He uses it to strip the tail from the

tailbone and, with a few more cuts around the muzzle, slickly yanks off the coon's hide. The time elapsed is a bit over the minute flat he was hoping for, but Robby, Sam, and Carrot Coon leave the stage to warm applause.

Lucy, a black Labrador retriever, reluctantly sits still for a portrait. She would much rather be wet and in motion, retrieving a downed duck.

Don Jackson and his dog, Lucy, wait for a morning flight along Island Creek.

*Lucy retrieves a mallard
duck downed by her master,
Don Jackson. The Labrador
retriever is a popular breed
for waterfowl hunters.*

OPPOSITE: *Island Creek
reflects the sunrise over
a classic Dorchester scene of
marsh and loblolly pine.*

Archaeologist Darrin Lowery searches for the history of the bay's original peoples along the edge of the Little Chop-tank River.

The EDGE

IT'S A FINE MAY DAY in the year 2000, ospreys peeping on their nests, the rising sun sparkling on the calm waters of Slaughter Creek in the northeastern corner of the Great Marsh. It's a good time to think about time, as archaeologist Darrin Lowery guides our skiff on a voyage that by noon will cover a few miles, and thousands of years.

We're skimming over a creek channel some ten feet below us. But a few hundred feet below that, Lowery says, is the paleochannel, the course the Susquehanna River followed a quarter-million years ago. For most of the time between then and now, the last Ice Age gripped North America. Glaciers bound up enough of the oceans' water that the sea level was hundreds of feet lower than at present. The Susquehanna carved a new gorge that would become the channel of today's Chesapeake, which is only the latest in a series of bays that have come and gone during millions of years of continental freezes and melts.

Only about 10,000 years ago did a warming trend refill the seas enough to begin backing up the Susquehanna in its valley to form what we know as our Chesapeake. This most recent version of the bay reached somewhere near its present level a few thousand years ago. It is not surprising, then, that the "timeless" landscape of the Great Marsh is geologically youthful. Scientists who have extracted cores of peat and radiocarbon-dated them, find that most formed within the last 2,000 years. Some peat is still forming as I write this.

We're headed with Lowery for Holland Point, where Slaughter Creek meets the Little Choptank River. The shoreline there is dense with big, handsome oyster shells, hardly an uncommon sight in these parts. A casual passerby might assume it was the former site of a seafood

oysters. Eventually the stone fragmented from the heat, forming telltale fractures. Other rocks, cracked like an onion unpeeling, were boiling stones, heated and put in pots to cook stews.

Since 1992, when he began exploring Slaughter Creek, Lowery has picked up close to a thousand arrowheads in one 200-yard stretch of Holland Point. Here and elsewhere along the edges of the Great Marsh, he's found an array of stone tools. He shows us "the Native American version of the Swiss Army knife," a chunk of rhyolite from which other, smaller tools could be flaked off. The chunk itself has a blade that, judging by the grooves in it, was a well-used oyster knife.

He shows another find: a five- to six-pound stone, drilled for use as a weight to hold fishnets in place. Like the oyster opener, it is identical in function, and not that far removed in form, from what current denizens of the Great Marsh

loading dock or a packinghouse. But Lowery knows it is nothing less than a fantastic window on the broad sweep of human habitation of the bay.

From among the shells, he scoops up small fragments of irregularly shaped stones, deep red to black in color. This is classic "fire-cracked" rock, he says. Native Americans brought cobblestones from riverbeds to line pits for roasting

This mortar and pestle were used to grind nuts, seeds, and wild grains into flour meal from 5,000 to 500 years ago. Even though corn is used in this photo, there is very little archaeological evidence that it was grown by the prehistoric peoples on Maryland's Eastern Shore prior to European contact.

A stone projectile point made of crystal quartz was used to tip a light spear for hunting from 4,000 to 2,000 years ago.

OPPOSITE: *A stone cache blade or knife, approximately 2,000 years old, was used as a cutting and scraping tool. Smaller cutting tools were flaked from its surface, a prehistoric version of the Swiss Army knife. This blade is made of rhyolite, a nonlocal stone material that was traded to the Delmarva area.*

still use every day. Holland Point, Lowery has deduced, was continuously inhabited by Native Americans from 3,000 years ago to the seventeenth century.

It is humbling to think that "primitive" cultures flourished in this spot for more than ten times as long as there has been a United States of America. Holland Point is an archaeologist's dream, essentially "a solid mass of prehistoric garbage," Lowery says. Such sites, he says, tend to be "oyster-biased." The calcium-rich shells of oysters neutralize acids in the soil that would otherwise quickly destroy most traces of bones and teeth.

Looking down at the modern garbage littering the shore—yellow polypropylene rope, Styrofoam crab-pot corks, nylon fishnet, and plastic wadding from duck hunters' expended

Though the function of this pop-eyed birdstone is unknown, it is thought to be about 2,000 years old. Only four or five similar objects have ever been found in the Chesapeake region. This artifact is made of hematite; similar pieces were called "birdstones" because they resemble a bird seated within a nest.

shotgun shells—Lowery reflects: "There's no doubt what some archaeologist who examines our artifacts is going to call this, the Petroleum Age."

Slaughter Creek is most valuable archaeologically, he says, for the span of time covered by several sites along its shoreline. They range from early colonial times back to 11,000 years ago, when the bay was just a river raging between cliffs more than a hundred feet high. "Because the Bay was ever changing as sea level rose, it holds a whole sweep of history—different peoples, different times, making their living different ways . . . here we have the whole continuum."

One site is especially interesting in that it was inhabited only for a short while, some 8,500 years ago, and contains tools and projectile points "very specific to a time we don't know much about. There are sites in Tennessee 8,500 years old with identical tools," Lowery says.

After casually tossing around millennia all morning, it comes as a shock to hear Lowery talk about his "race against time" to study archaeological sites around the Great Marsh. But erosion, driven by a sea-level rise that has accelerated dramatically in the last century or so, has already shredded lots of what he has found since 1992. Holland Point, he thinks, will be gone beneath the waves within five years.

"You could do so much in this place, but there's more money and interest in the historic than the prehistoric. If these sites had a famous person associated with them, I'd guarantee they'd be preserved. It gets into questions of whose history you choose to preserve—a few colonial notables, or eleven thousand years of Dorchester Joe Schmoes?"

This stone anchor or pound-net weight with counter-sunk hole for a rope is made from a large, heavy piece of basalt and is 500 to 3,000 years old. It may have functioned as an anchor or a weight for the crib or head portion of a prehistoric pound net.

Not that far removed from the prehistoric pound-net weight, old bricks are used to anchor a modern fisherman's net.

Charles Woodland and
Chris Jones remove fish from
one of their pound nets in
Fishing Bay. Modern-day
pound nets are thought to be
quite similar to those in use
hundreds, even thousands, of
years ago.

OPPOSITE: *A crew member aboard the* Lisa Tina *loads the catch from a pound net, mostly croakers, into bushel baskets.*

Chris Jones holds the big catch of the day, a black drum.

OVERLEAF: *Hoopersville, a watermen's village on Hooper's Island, seems to float between the sky and the waters of the Honga River on a calm August morning.*

A net-maker's needle hangs from a length of nylon during the building of a pound net near Crocheron.

RIGHT: *As generations of his family have done before, Donald Mills makes a pound net in his front yard near Crocheron. Today, Mills buys lengths of net and sews them into the proper configuration to suit the fishermen's needs, but he has memories of his family tying the thousands of knots that go into making a single pound net.*

The paint on an abandoned building near Toddville may be fading, but the sentiment of the former occupant still rings true.

With bright red paint, an old packinghouse at Crocheron harbor stands out against the low marsh grasses and blue sky.

Surrounded by marsh grasses, Matt Mullen runs along Phillips Gunning Club Road. The Karen Noonan Center, in a former gun club, is in the background.

Students from the Karen Noonan Center put this sign along the road that leads to the environmental education center run by the Chesapeake Bay Foundation in the old Phillips Gunning Club. During some wind and tide combinations, the road is under several inches of water, creating a virtual island.

*The final resting place of
Sarah Bloodsworth on her
namesake island has become
a favorite nesting area of
great blue herons.*

A brown pelican nest sits inches above the high-tide line on a small island.

A newly hatched brown pelican sits quietly in his nest and shows little concern over a visitor.

A young brown pelican thrusts its head down its parent's gullet in search of partially digested fish.

His eyes on the prize, a brown pelican makes a ka-mikaze dive into Hooper Straits.

111

*Down is giving way to
primary feathers on these
month-old brown pelicans.*

A canoeist pokes along the edge of Chicone Creek, a tributary of the Nanticoke River, near Vienna, Maryland. The creek's water-shed was the site of one of the last settlements of the Nanticoke Indians.

MONARCHS

John has never studied Greek
but he knows the Chesapeake.

GILBERT BYRON, *River Schooling*

YOU STUDY NATURE your whole life, then see
something entirely new in a place you've been a
hundred times. That's how it is when I happen
on the miracle bush.

I've been paddling the edge of a river draining the Great Marsh for half an hour one afternoon when I become aware of another river
flowing over and around my kayak. It's a proces-
sion of Monarchs, the annual migration that
funnels the butterflies from across eastern
North America to a few winter roosts in central
Mexico, so sequestered that scientists searched
nearly half a century before finding them in
1975.

It's the first day of fall, brisk and blowy. The
tide is ebbing, exposing a couple feet of rich,
brown marsh bank, topped by thick ranks of
spartina grasses that toss and gleam in the late
afternoon sun. Tucked under the lee of the
bank, I glide in near calm, watching the north
wind splay dark cats-paws out across the river,
building to whitecaps in the channel.

The Monarchs follow the edge too, handling
twenty-knot gusts with the aplomb of falcons.
They fly singly, or in pairs and threes. All afternoon I never see more than a dozen of them at
once, but there is never a moment when several
aren't in sight. They are moving considerably
faster than the five miles an hour I manage in a
kayak, frequently flitting several yards out over
the water, then tacking inland, then down the
edge.

It looks inefficient. But we, who send me-
chanical probes to the moons of Jupiter, know
little about how an insect weighing less than a
gram, with orange and black-veined wings deli-

A marsh periwinkle climbs up a stalk of Spartina alterniflora, *harvesting algae and detritus from the grass's surface. These tiny snails climb the stalks of marsh grass as the tide rises and descend as the water level falls.*

cate as tissue paper, navigates from Maine to Mexico. None of the sojourners brightly flickering down the edges of the Great Marsh this day have any acquaintance with where they are unerringly headed, for mountain valleys ten thousand feet high, fifteen hundred miles away.

They are generations removed from the Monarchs that last spring mated and reproduced and died in the highlands west of Mexico City, spawning successive waves of offspring that did the same, leapfrogging their species north all summer across the continent. The onset of chilly weather has arrested this cycle, delayed sexual maturity in these autumn travelers, who will instead put their energy into traveling south to restart the whole grand show next spring.

Some scientists believe the origins of the Monarchs' migratory phenomenon lie in the retreat of the last Ice Age ten thousand years ago, when glacial melt also boosted the sea level and formed Chesapeake Bay. Plants expanded their range north, including milkweed, the only vegetation on which Monarch females lay their eggs. Over millennia, the theory goes, the butterflies followed.

The sun is setting, and I'm tired, but something draws me to paddle another quarter-mile or so down the marsh edge. Perhaps, although I

As the morning sun warms their wings, Monarch butterflies leave a high-tide bush and continue their journey south.

knew the Monarchs were going to Mexico, I am curious where they will go that evening. They become lethargic once temperatures drop near 55 degrees Fahrenheit, and clearly it is getting time for them to pack it in.

From maybe fifteen yards offshore I see nothing but endless acres of spartinas and one little clump of *Iva frutescens*, the marsh elder, or high-tide bush. One of the common shrubs of the bay edge, Iva is most unprepossessing. Its dull little leaves show no fall color, and its fruits and flowers are barely discernible (they do have a faint, minty odor when crushed). A twiggy shrub seldom exceeding a few feet high in the marshes around here, it is somewhat useful for campfire kindling and for camouflaging duck blinds if nothing else is available.

A man who grew up in the marsh on Smith Island told me that out there they call Iva "miracle bush." It is considered, he chuckled, "a miracle anything grows out here at all." Out of ecological correctness, I take it on faith that Iva is necessary for something, but I have never been sure what it was.

The flow of Monarchs has slowed to a trickle, and the light is beginning to fade. Turning for home, I notice that the little Iva bush on the shore seems to quiver. And its color is not quite right, more dun than lackluster green. On

Monarch butterflies blanket
a high-tide bush (Iva
frutescens) in the Great
Marsh as they rest during
their migration south.

closer inspection—miracle of miracle bushes—the little clump turns out to be virtually cloaked in Monarchs, hundreds of them, wings folded back for the night to expose their duller underside. Layer upon layer, the weary migrants drape every twig-end and branch of the marsh shrub in living velvet.

Even minor discovery is thrilling. I can appreciate the reaction of the explorers who finally came upon the great winter roosts of the Monarch in 1975. That first encounter, sun streaming into groves cloaked with tens of millions of butterflies, was "like walking into Chartres Cathedral and seeing light coming through stained glass windows . . . the eighth wonder of the world," one entomologist said.

And the discoverers coined a term for these roost areas, ranging from a few dozen to a few thousand trees, relatively tiny areas with micro-climates uniquely suited to the butterflies' survival. They called them "magic circles."

And here on the marsh, tossing in the north wind and the rich hues of late afternoon on the first day of fall, is a Chesapeake version of a magic circle. *Iva frutescens,* as way station for a few drops in this torrent of color and life that ripples across half the North American continent, never served so well nor looked so good.

I'm not done with the miracle bush, for in five decades of progging the marsh edge, I never saw the like, and may not again. The next morning I return with Dave Harp, cameras

A tiger swallowtail butterfly takes flight from a honeysuckle vine.

A canoeist enjoys a spectacu-
lar light show just before
the first dawn of a new year
on Hooper Straits.

waiting for sunrise to illuminate our minor miracle bush. The Monarchs are still there, hanging motionless in the calm and crystalline air. A red-winged blackbird's vibrato razzes the marsh. Terrapin heads peer up at us from the shallows, and a small striped bass jumps straight up. Out in the river a trotliner patrols his baited crab line, radio thumping to a local rock station.

Within five minutes of the sun's first kiss, a few wings begin unfolding. More minutes, and the Iva begins to wink a deep, bright orange, then to flicker and quiver and blossom—and flare as the first Monarchs go airborne at 7.15 A.M. One rises a few feet, loops the Iva once, then turns to follow the green edge—headed south by west, Maine to Mexico, coaxed and goaded by signals known only to itself, spreading beauty for all to see along its way, from miracle bush to magic circle.

OPPOSITE: *The ultimate edge dweller, a great blue heron is dwarfed by a salt marsh as he hunts for fish, crabs, small rodents, and other marsh inhabitants.*

Great blue herons greet the rising sun on Bloodsworth Island. Most of the island has been a bombing range for decades, but the northern tip has been designated a refuge for wildlife.

Rendered pink by the setting sun, Tundra swans fly over the old caretaker's house at a former hunting club near Crocheron. The house now serves as staff quarters for the Chesapeake Bay Foundation and the former gun club is an environmental education center.